To:

From:

motherhood

is not for sissies

Evelyn Beilenson

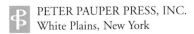

PETER PAUPER PRESS, INC.
White Plains, New York

For my mom, who was always there for me

Designed by Karine Syvertsen

Photo credits appear on page 72.

Copyright © 2005
Peter Pauper Press, Inc.
202 Mamaroneck Avenue
White Plains, NY 10601
ISBN 1-59359-975-7
Printed in China
7 6 5 4 3

Visit us at peterpauper.com

motherhood

is not for sissies

introduction

motherhood is not for sissies. A mother needs strength, courage, patience, a big heart, and, most of all, a good sense of humor. Raising children is not for the fainthearted; they disturb your sleep, add wrinkles to your brow, and test the limits of your physical endurance. Who else but a mother can press forty pounds of toddler in one arm while making dinner with the other—and singing the alphabet to boot?

And yet, at the end of the day, there is no other work (every mother is a working mother) that is quite as satisfying. The smile and the hug are the best "thank you" a mother can receive.

And then those toddlers become teens. That's what Ed Asner probably had in mind when he said that "raising kids is part joy and part guerrilla warfare."

This Keepsake is dedicated to all mothers. We hope the images and messages in the following pages will make you smile, ruefully perhaps, as you face the daily hair-raising but humorous events that define motherhood.

E. B.

Think of stretch marks as pregnancy service stripes.

JOYCE ARMOR

7

Life is tough
enough without
having someone
kick you from
the inside.

RITA RUDNER

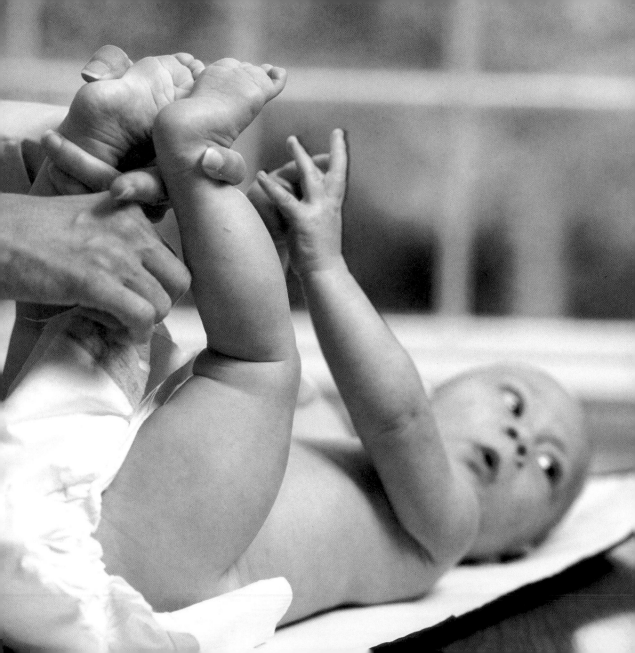

Laughter is like changing a baby's diaper. It doesn't permanently solve any problems, but it makes things more acceptable for a while.

AUTHOR UNKNOWN

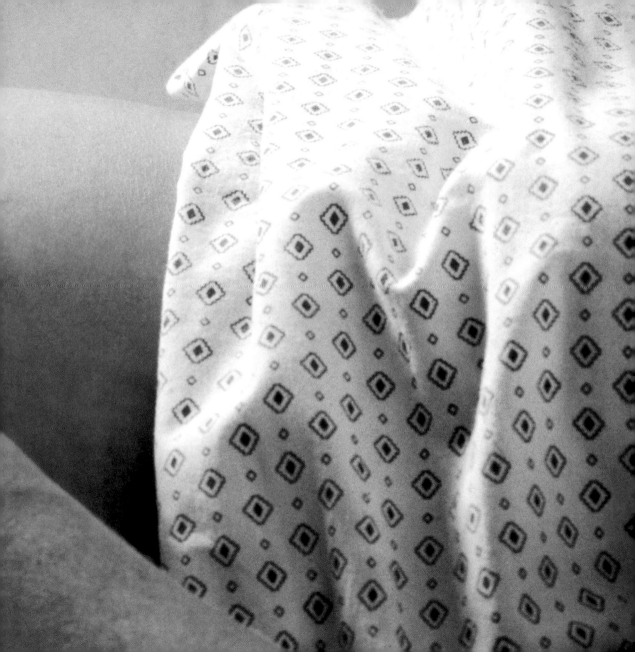

I don't know why they
say "you have a baby."
The baby has *you*.

GALLAGHER

A mother is a person who, seeing there are only four pieces of pie for five people, promptly announces she never did care for pie.

TENNEVA JORDAN

Motherhood is a first aid kit for healing our hurts, worries, and mishaps.

The most effective
form of birth control
I know is spending
the day with my kids.

JILL BENSLEY

Surrendering to mother-hood means surrendering to interruption.

Erica Jong

23

All mothers are working mothers.

AUTHOR UNKNOWN

A suburban mother's role is to
deliver children obstetrically once,
and by car forever after.

PETER DE VRIES

I figure if the kids are alive at the end of the day, I've done my job.

ROSEANNE

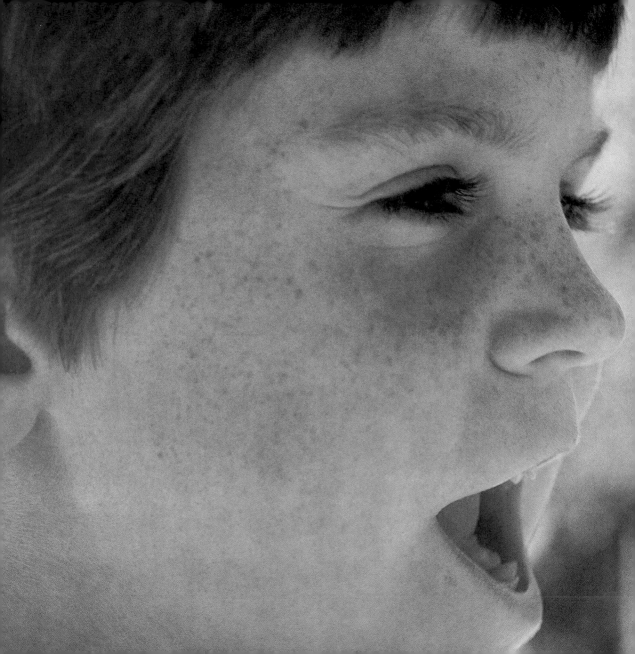

Motherhood is not *for the fa018thearted. Used frogs, skinned knees, and the insults of teenage girls are not meant for the wimpy.*

DANIELLE STEELE

Enlightenment is the quiet acceptance that one day your children will grow up—and leave.

Babies don't come with directions on the back or batteries that can be removed. Motherhood is twenty-four hours a day, seven days a week. You can't "leave the office."

PATRICIA SCHROEDER

*With kids,
life's always a
"beach."*

That million-dollar smile doesn't come cheap.

*Never tell a child
anything you wouldn't
want the whole
neighborhood to know.*

A mother who navigates the waters of the terrible twos can weather any storm.

Child rearing means

taking a big bite

out of your life.

Cleaning your house
while your kids are
still growing is like
shoveling the walk
before it stops snowing.

PHYLLIS DILLER

*Ask your child what
he wants for dinner
only if he is buying.*

FRAN LEBOWITZ

Who said tackling motherhood would be glamorous?

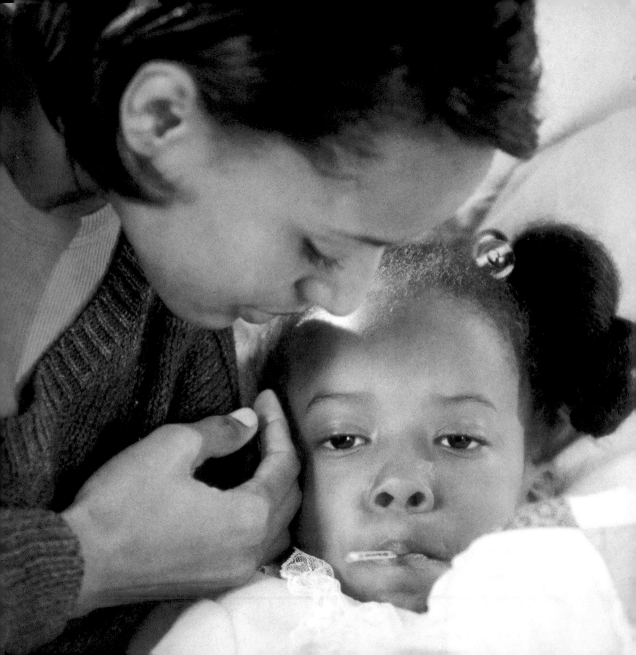

There are only two things
a child will share willingly—
communicable diseases
and his mother's age.

BENJAMIN SPOCK

Children wear out
their mothers faster
than their shoes.

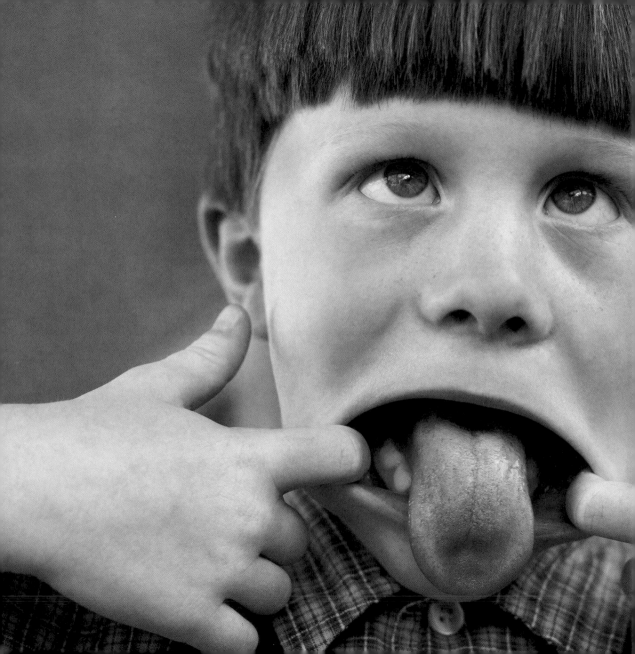

Insanity is hereditary; you get it from your children.

*My mother had a great
deal of trouble with me,
but I think she enjoyed it.*

MARK TWAIN

In the cycles of motherhood, there is never a dull moment.

Darwin actually had mothers in mind when he came up with the "survival of the fittest" theory.

*If there were no schools
to take the children
away from home
part of the time,
the insane asylums
would be filled
with mothers.*

E. W. HOWE

*Life begins when the kids
(and the grownups!)
go to bed.*

Many old-fashioned theories of raising children no longer hold water.

When all else fails,
pray.

Photo Credits

Cover Photo: © Stone/Getty Images

Pages 1 and 3: © RubberBall
    Productions/Getty Images

Page 5: © Linda Syvertsen

Pages 6-7: © comstock.com

Pages 8-9: © Digital Vision/Getty Images

Page 10: © CORBIS

Pages 12-13: © comstock.com

Page 15: © Alyssa Weisberg

Pages 16-17: © Image Bank

Page 19: © comstock.com

Page 20: © Jennifer Gallan

Pages 22-23: © Thinkstock/Getty Images

Page 24: © Marc Carter/Image Bank

Pages 26-27: © Colin Barker/Image Bank

Page 29: © Photodisc/Getty Images

Pages 30-31: © Photodisc/Getty Images

Page 33: © Photodisc/Getty Images

Page 34: © Martha Zschock

Pages 36-37: © Photodisc/Getty
    Images

Pages 38-39: © comstock.com

Page 41: © comstock.com

Pages 42-43: © comstock.com

Page 45: © Brand X Pictures

Page 46: © CORBIS

Page 49: © CORBIS

Pages 50-51: © CORBIS

Page 52: © comstock.com

Page 55: © Valerie Parker

Pages 56-57: © RubberBall
    Productions/Getty Images

Page 59: © Daly & Newton/Image Bank

Pages 60-61: © Ed Kashi/CORBIS

Page 62: © comstock.com

Pages 64-65: © Digital Vision/Getty Images

Page 66: © Photodisc/Getty Images

Pages 68-69: © Thinkstock/Getty Images

Page 70: © Photodisc/Getty Images